FIRST 100 DAYS

CONTRACT WITH AMERICA
(ILLUSTRATED)

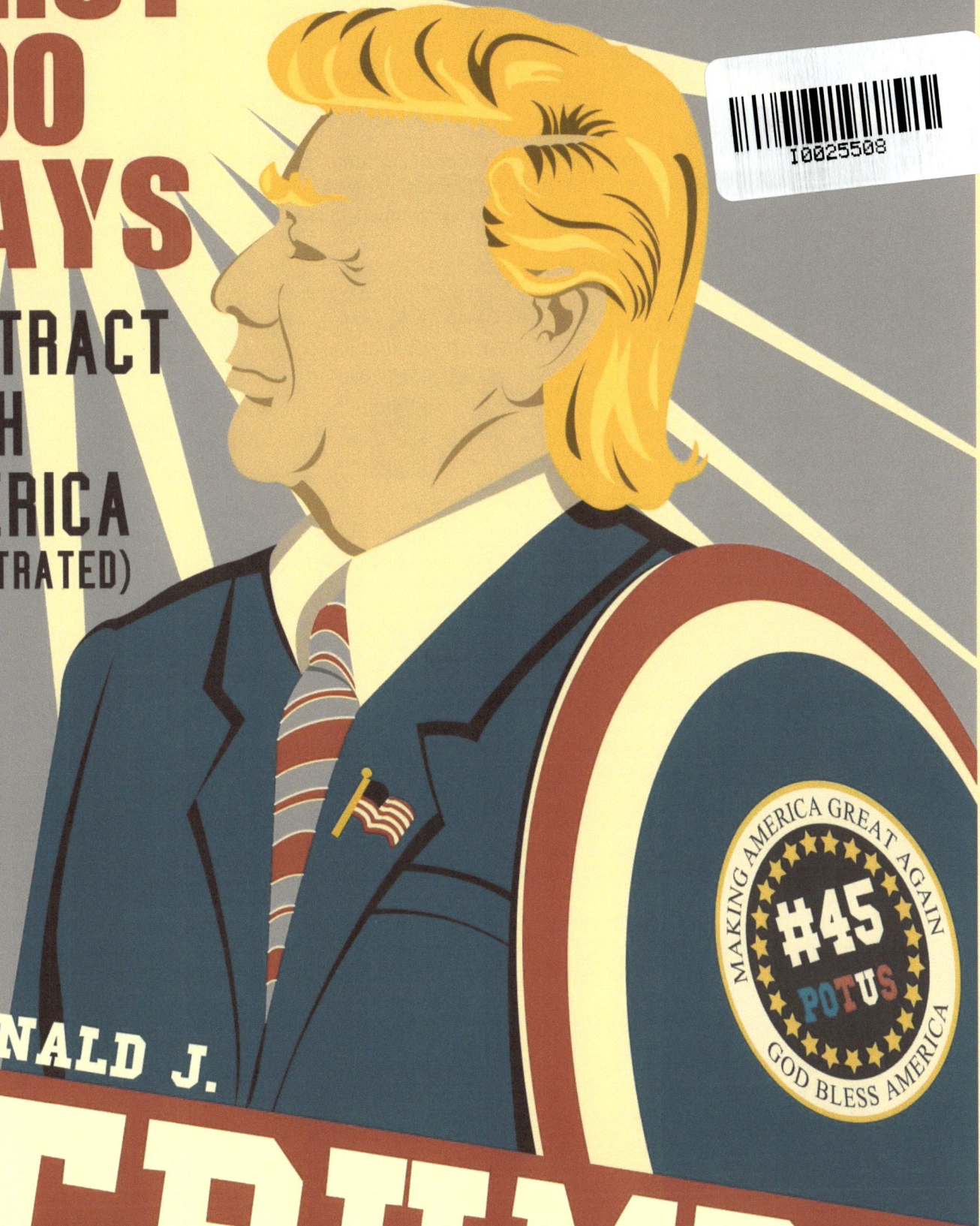

BY ELIZABETH LITTLE
& ELLEN SALLAS

DONALD J.

TRUMP

MAKING AMERICA GREAT AGAIN

#45

POTUS

GOD BLESS AMERICA

Donald J. Trump
First 100 Days: Contract with America
Copyright 2017 Ellen Sallas
Illustrations by Ellen Sallas and Elizabeth Little
All rights reserved.

ISBN-13: 978-0692831281
ISBN-10: 0692831282
Little Roni Publishers / Byhalia, MS
www.littleronipublishers.com
@LittleRoniPublishers

RESOURCES NOTE: In this book, the text for every illustrated page will begin with one of the points from this historic document. **The authors have placed President Trump's points in bold font,** sometimes paraphrased for space and/or flow. All credit for these points goes to the free downloadable PDF from
https://assets.donaldjtrump.com/CONTRACT_FOR_THE_VOTER.pdf .

INTERIOR ILLUSTRATIONS: The illustrations are hand-drawn by Ellen Sallas, then digitally recreated, stroke-by-stroke, and colored by graphic designer Elizabeth Little using Photoshop InDesign™. All art is original to the illustrators; note three pieces of "Derivative Art" (license acquired from copyright holder): "Hiring Freeze" artwork derived from vector designed by ÁRTICA (Jesús Sanz, CreativeMarket.com), "Restrictions on Becoming Lobbyists" artwork derived from © Canstockphoto.com /siraanamwong, "Improve Education Options" artwork derived from vector Designed by Freepik.com. Note one Licensed photograph: "Trump at Podium Intro Page" artwork derived from photo image ©Gage Skidmore www.gageskidmore.com

DISCLAIMERS: Neither of the authors have been financially or otherwise endorsed by any political party. This book (and its sister coloring book edition) are purely works of the authors themselves, and the opinions expressed therein are theirs alone and do not reflect those of the publishers or producers.

SYNOPSIS: This is an illustrated exposition on the historic document "Contract with the American Voter," by Donald J. Trump, made available on his website at www.DonaldJTrump.com. Each point or promise is illustrated and explained below in simplified text for readers of all ages.

EDUCATORS: This book is available from the publisher at bulk prices. Email submissionsLRP@gmail.com for information and to order.

AUTHOR WEBSITES: www.EllenCMaze.com & www.MyPresidentStickers.com
Twitter: @Ellenmaze @ConservSNARK
Facebook: www.facebook.com/ellen.maze

PUBLISHED IN THE UNITED STATES OF AMERICA

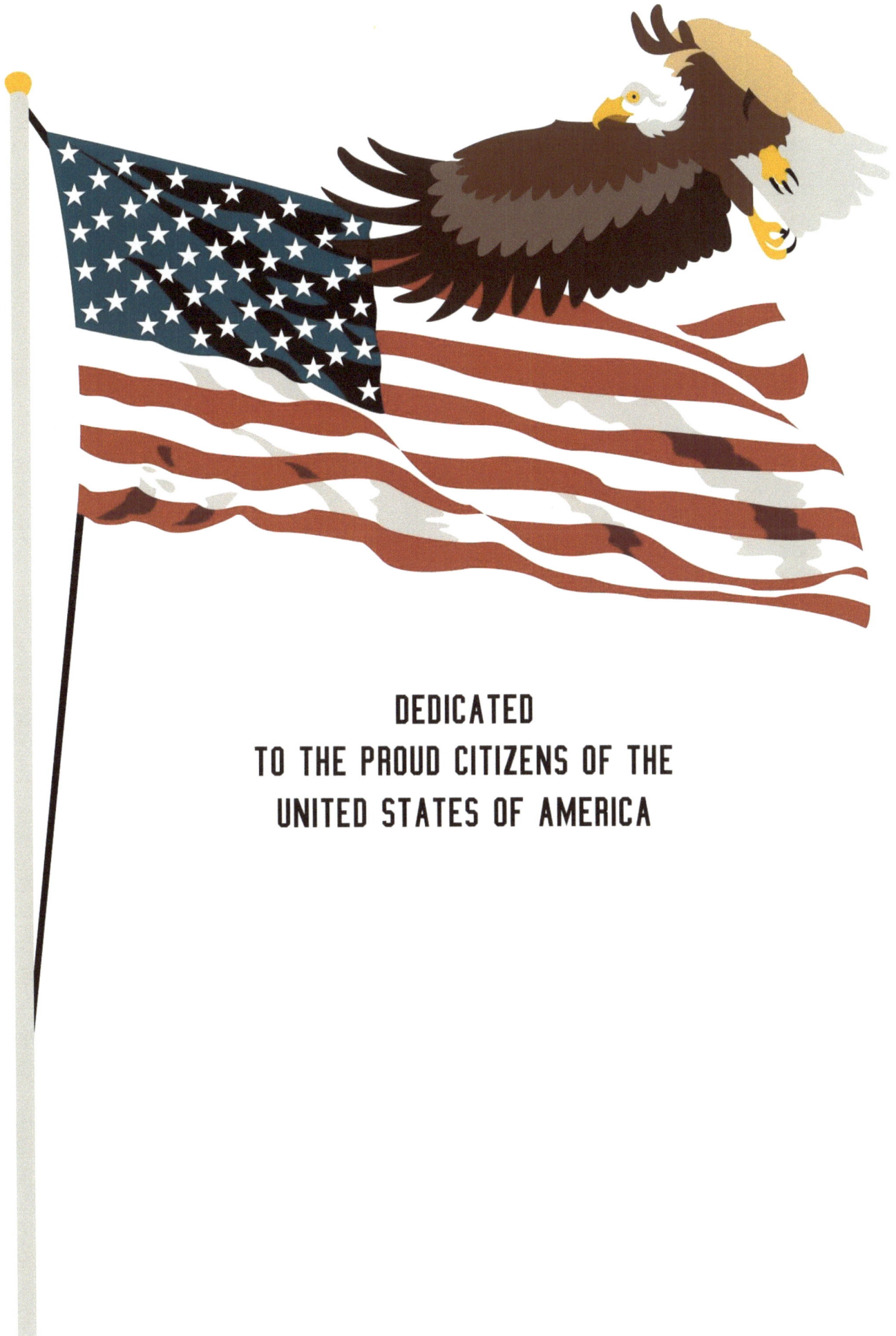

DEDICATED
TO THE PROUD CITIZENS OF THE
UNITED STATES OF AMERICA

HIRING FREEZE
ON FEDERAL EMPL

LABEL CHINA
A CURRENCY
MANIPULATOR

RESTRICTIONS
ON BECOMING
LOBBYISTS

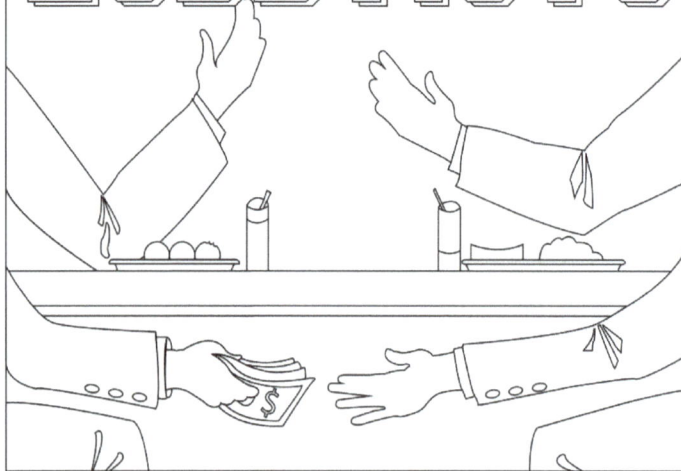

President Trump will propose a 5-year ban on White House and Congressional officials becoming lobbyists after they leave government service, a lifetime ban on White House officials lobbying on behalf of a foreign government, and a complete ban on foreign lobbyists raising money for American elections. Being able to profit financially or materially from past government service creates an environment of temptation and corruption, evidenced by the veritable "swamp of scandals" our in which our current Federal Government wallows.[7]

LIMIT
ERMS
FOR CONGRESS

The authors have created a coloring book version as well.
Purchase yours at bookstores worldwide,
or at these websites:
www.Amazon.com
www.EllenCMaze.com
www.MyPresidentStickers.com

FIRST 100 DAYS

CONTRACT WITH AMERICA

DONALD J. TRUMP

On October 22, 2016, in Gettysburg, PA, then-Presidential candidate Donald J. Trump introduced a groundbreaking "first 100 days" action plan, *Contract with the American Voter*, to put America back on the path to greatness. President Trump asks the citizens of this nation to dream big and have faith in the greatness of the American character. In this book, the text for every illustrated page will begin with one of the points from this historic document. **The authors have placed President Trump's points in bold font,** sometimes paraphrased for space and/or flow. All credit for these points goes to the free downloadable PDF from https://assets.donaldjtrump.com/CONTRACT_FOR_THE_VOTER.pdf.

In the words of President Donald J. Trump: "What follows is my 100-day action plan to Make America Great Again. It is a contract between Donald J. Trump and the American voter – and begins with restoring honesty, accountability and change to Washington."

This Contract with the American Voter begins with...

LIMIT TERMS

FOR CONGRESS

...proposing a Constitutional Amendment to impose term limits on all members of **Congress.** Currently, The United States Congress is made up of the Senate (each state has two senators, which equals 100) and the House of Representatives (435 members). Senators have terms of 6-years, Representatives have 2-year terms.[2] Senators can be re-elected indefinitely, as there is no limit for the number of terms that a senator can serve in the United States government.[3]

HIRING FREEZE
ON FEDERAL EMPLOYEES

President Trump will propose a hiring freeze on federal employees (exempting military, public safety, and public health) **to reduce federal workforce through attrition.** The Bureau of Labor Statistics data shows that those employed by government in the USA in August of this year outnumbered those employed in the manufacturing sector by almost 1.8-one.[4]   The implication is that many of these jobs are unnecessary with a single full-time workload split between six, seven and even eight employees in some instances across the nation. This duplicative employment trend often leads to poor performance and wastes the taxpayers' money.[5]

FEDERAL REGULATIONS

CUT 2 FOR EVERY 1

President Trump will propose a requirement that for every new federal regulation, two existing regulations must be eliminated. Passing hundreds of new laws a year results in mandates, regulations, taxes, subsidies and transfer programs that hurt American productivity, private and commercial business commerce and economy, and unjustly infringe on the individual rights of citizens.[6]

RESTRICTIONS ON BECOMING LOBBYISTS

President Trump will propose a 5-year ban on White House and Congressional officials becoming lobbyists after they leave government service, a lifetime ban on White House officials lobbying on behalf of a foreign government, and a complete ban on foreign lobbyists raising money for American elections. Being able to profit financially or materially from past government service creates an environment of temptation and corruption, evidenced by the veritable "swamp of scandals" in which our current Federal Government wallows.[7]

RENEGOTIATE
NAFTA

Renegotiate or withdraw from NAFTA. The North American Free Trade Agreement (1994), is an agreement signed by Canada, Mexico, and the United States, creating a trilateral trade bloc in North America.[8] Since its implementation, the American economy has suffered dangerous and toxic imports, as well as an influx of illegal immigrants. Under NAFTA, we have seen a 300% increase of illegal immigrants in the U.S. and watched 300,000 American family farms go out of business. NAFTA does not benefit the American worker, but encourages our jobs to leave the country in pursuit of lower wage rates, non-existent environmental standards, and trade without restrictions.[9]

WITHDRAW FROM THE

TPP

Withdraw from the Trans-Pacific Partnership. This agreement creates a trade zone with lower tariffs/taxes for twelve Pacific member nations—the US, Japan, Malaysia, Vietnam, Singapore, Brunei, Australia, New Zealand, Canada, Mexico, Chile, and Peru—12 countries accounting for 40% of the global economy. Opponents of the TPP say this new trading alliance would allow American firms to more easily move jobs overseas to take advantage of cheap, foreign labor. Or, conversely, American employers could keep jobs here in the US, but at lower wages.[10] In addition, the TPP would have rewritten global rules on intellectual property enforcement, and not in a way that benefits Americans.[11]

LABEL CHINA A CURRENCY MANIPULATOR

Direct the Secretary of the Treasury to label China a currency manipulator. China manipulates its currency by buying U.S. government debt with an unending supply of newly printed money. This floods the market with Chinese currency and increases demand for American dollars. According to many estimates, Chinese government intervention keeps the yuan approximately 20 percent below its free market value against the dollar.[12] In labeling China as such, President Trump can apply countervailing duties to China and "any country that devalues its currency to gain unfair advantage over the U.S."[13]

IDENTIFY & END FOREIGN TRADE ABUSES

¡Adiós! ACME is moving to Mexico.

Direct the Secretary of Commerce and U.S. Trade Representative to identify and end foreign trading abuses. The illustration above reflects a common trade abuse of moving a company out of the U.S. to save money. President Trump will work deals and/or impose tariffs and taxes to keep companies in the U.S., making it more expensive for them to leave than to stay. Trade Deals like NAFTA and TPP do not put American workers first, and under President Trump, the American worker would get first chance at all jobs. Up until now, politicians and corporations create abusive trade deals to make money, without concern for the average American worker suffering under these deals.[14]

LIFT RESTRICTIONS ON U.S. ENERGY RESERVES

Lift restrictions on the production of $50 trillion dollars' worth of job-producing American energy reserves, including shale, oil, natural gas and clean coal. U.S. oil production doubled between 2008 and 2015 due purely to American ingenuity and persistence, despite the Obama administration's federal energy policy actively hindering this work every step of the way. Obama's Department of the Interior cancelled oil and gas lease sales early in his first term,[15] and in 2011, they blocked access to most of America's offshore oil and gas reserves, placing a de facto moratorium on drilling.[16]

MOVE VITAL ENERGY PROJECTS

FORWARD

Lift the Obama-Clinton roadblocks in order to move vital energy infrastructure projects forward. A good example is the Keystone Pipeline XL, a Canada-based project that would deliver up to 830,000 barrels of oil per day to Gulf Coast refineries without posing a significant environmental risk, nor contribute substantially to carbon dioxide emissions. Regardless to political posturing, environmental impact statements have published that the pipeline's climate effects would be minimal.[17]

Cancel billions of dollars in payments to U.N. Many scientists and American voters believe the dire urgency to stop using natural resources and the human-causal factor touted by the Left is overblown and outright deceptive. One example, in April, 2016, the U.S. and 170 other nations, signed the Paris Agreement on climate change, where countries invest billions, while promising to move away from using natural resources such as coal, natural gas, and oil.[18] Allowing other countries to dictate U.S. energy policy is not good for Americans. Protecting our environment is important, and President Trump will ensure we do so without spending more money on other countries than our own.

SPEND
ON AMERICAN
ENVIRONMENTAL
NEEDS

...and use the money to fix America's water and environmental infrastructure. Some of our infrastructure issues are water scarcity[19]; congested high-traffic expressways (causing millions of hours delay per year)[20]; aging high-traffic bridges in desperate need of repair (such as the Brooklyn Bridge with repairs grossly over budget and still not completed)[21]; our canals, waterways, and locks; our interstate road systems; our underground municipal water systems; our factory emissions situation; and the list goes on and on. President Trump believes *American* climate needs trump those of foreign nations, and a balance of giving away and investing at home needs to be reached to put America FIRST.

CANCEL
UNCONSTITUTIONAL
Executive Actions

Cancel every unconstitutional executive action, memorandum and order issued by President Obama. From the controversial Dream Act[22] blindly granting amnesty to millions of illegal aliens, to mandating special liberties be given to one subset of the population over another, Barack Obama's "pen and phone"[23] have left the majority of working class Americans feeling discriminated against and disenfranchised.[24] President Trump has made it plain that many issues will be sent to the states to decide (such as gay marriage and legalizing marijuana)[25], which is part of the drive to shrink the federal government.

SELECT
A CONSTITUTION-UPHOLDING SUPREME COURT JUSTICE

Begin the process of selecting a judge who will uphold and defend the Constitution of the United States. With the death of conservative justice Antonin Scalia in February, 2016, the Supreme Court will need a new member to complete the customary nine sitting justices. With Justice Kennedy at 80 years old and Justice Ginsburg at 83, President Trump may have two spots to fill before long. If and when this occurs, it would appear that the Supreme Court would see a 6-3 conservative majority.[26] Conservative Americans hope this quells the erosion of the "Traditional American Way of Life" experienced during the Obama Administration.

CANCEL
FEDERAL FUNDING 4
SANCTUARY CITIES

Sanctuary City
Welcome Illegal
Immigrants!

→
EXIT

Cancel all federal funding to Sanctuary Cities. American voters want to see an end to all sanctuary cites and have the federal government enforce the immigration laws.[27] A sanctuary city is a place illegal aliens can find shelter from the Law, and although the term sounds pious enough, too often these illegal aliens commit violent crimes against American citizens and escape justice because of lax law enforcement. Cities that refuse to uphold immigration laws under President Trump will lose federal funding. It is better for America if our laws are considered sacrosanct by all people, citizen or not.

REMOVE MORE THAN 2MILLION

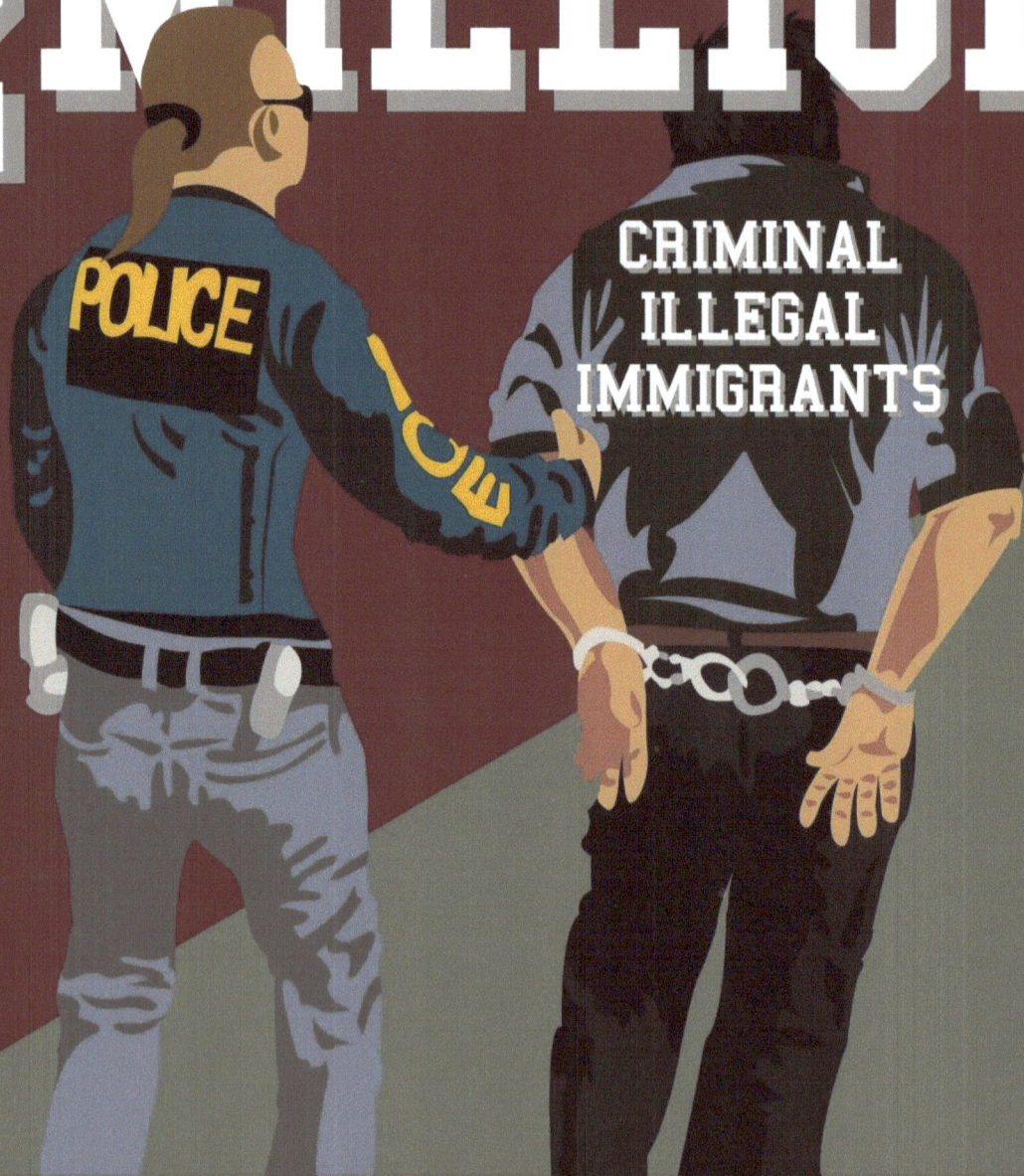

CRIMINAL ILLEGAL IMMIGRANTS

POLICE

Begin removing the more than 2 million criminal illegal immigrants from the country and cancel visas to foreign countries that won't take them back. President Trump has said that his priority (in all matters) is the well-being and prosperity of 300 million American citizens FIRST. Deporting known criminal illegal immigrants is the first move.[28] On working Day One, January 23, 2017, White House Press Secretary Sean Spicer assured the Press that President Trump's focus and priority was to first deal with these violent and dangerous people first.

SUSPEND IMMIGRATION FROM TERROR-PRONE REGIONS

Suspend immigration from terror-prone regions where vetting cannot safely occur. The Global Terrorism Index Report of 2016-2017 ranks Iraq, Afghanistan, Nigeria, and Syria as the top four countries from which terrorists originate, based upon per-year counts of terrorist incidents, fatalities, and injuries.[29] It should be common sense to be careful about who the United States allows within her borders, but current policy has failed us.

INTRODUCE
THE FOLLOWING
LEGISLATIVE MEASURES

MIDDLE-CLASS TAX RELIEF
& SIMPLIFICATION ACT

President Trump will fight for the passage of the Middle Class Tax Relief And Simplification Act. This is an economic plan designed to grow the economy and create millions of new jobs through tax reduction and simplification.[30] Tax simplification is a major part of President Trump's plan. Get deeper details at https://www.donaldjtrump.com/policies/tax-plan.

END THE OFFSHORING ACT

President Trump will end The Offshoring Act. This establishes tariffs that will discourage companies from laying off their workers in order to relocate in other countries. They will also not be able to ship their products back to the U.S. tax-free.[31] Offshoring American jobs has accelerated over the last decade and hit the American worker hard. In the past 14 years, the U.S. has lost more than 70,000 factories and 5 million manufacturing jobs.[32]

SPUR
INFRASTRUCTURE INVESTMENT

President Trump will push for the American Energy & Infrastructure Act. The American Society of Civil Engineers has identified a plethora of needs within our country's infrastructure, giving the nation a grade of D+, and projecting a needed investment of $3.6 trillion to begin repair.[33] The American Energy & Infrastructure Act is a plan to encourage through tax incentives, public and private investments directed at these issues.

IMPROVE

EDUCATION OPTIONS
FOR PARENTS & STUDENTS

President Trump will push the School Choice and Education Opportunity Act, which will redirect 20 million in education dollars in order to give parents the right to send their children to the school of their choice, be it public, private, magnet, charter, home, or else. Just as importantly, the act would end the controversial federal common core program and place education supervision responsibility onto the schools' local communities. Additionally, part of the plan is to expand vocational education and make 2 and 4-year college more affordable.

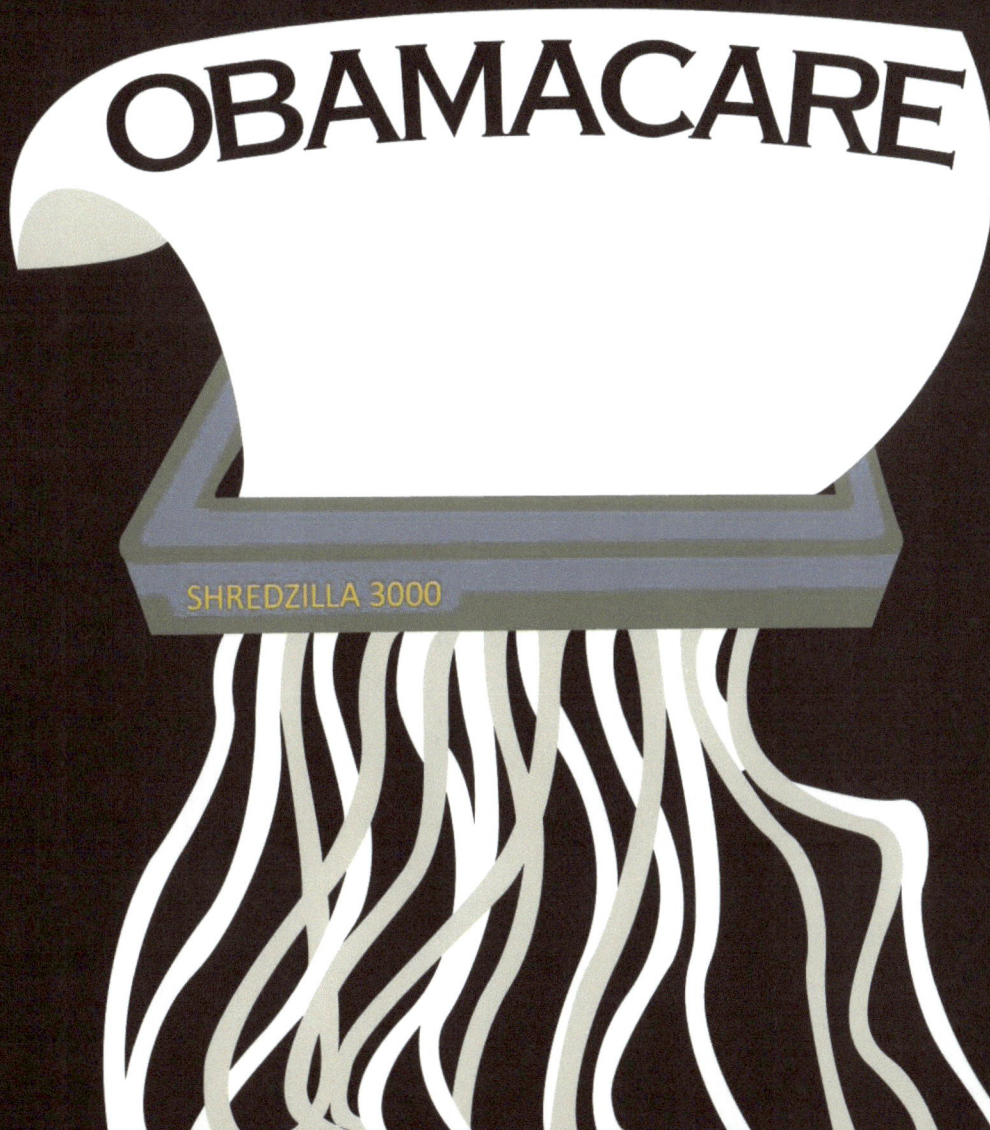

REPEAL&REPLACE

OBAMACARE

SHREDZILLA 3000

President Trump will work with Congress to immediately repeal and replace Obamacare. Once repealed, Health Savings Accounts would be instituted for those insured, Americans will be able to purchase health insurance across state lines, and the states will manage all Medicaid funds. President Trump's replacement plan also includes reforms that will cut the red tape preventing drug approval of life-saving medications.

VASTLY IMPROVE
CHILD & ELDER CARE
TAX DEDUCTIONS

President Trump will work to pass Affordable Childcare and Eldercare Act, which will provide tax breaks for citizens paying for this care and incentivizes employers to provide on-site childcare services. The plan provides for tax-free Dependent Care Savings Accounts with matching contributions for low-income families, as well as safe and affordable childcare for all.[34]

BUILD THE WALL

President Trump will push the End Illegal Immigration Act. This plan "Fully-funds the construction of a wall on our southern border with the full understanding that the country Mexico will be reimbursing the United States for the full cost of such wall."[35] The Act establishes mandatory minimum prison sentences for immigrants who re-enter the U.S. illegally after being deported. The GAO reports that in many states, more than 30% of homicides are committed by illegal immigrants.[36] There's also a provision that enhances penalties for immigrants who overstay their visas which ensures open jobs are available to American workers first.

REDUCE
CRIME & VIOLENCE
NATIONWIDE

President Trump will introduce the Restoring Community Safety Act to address surging crime, drug trafficking, and violence across our nation. The FBI's most recent "Crime in the United States" report reveals a 3.9% increase in violent crime, with an estimated 1.2M violent crimes committed around the nation.[37] The **Restoring Community Safety Act** creates a task force on violent crime and will ensure there is proper funding to train and assist local and federal law enforcement agencies to perform their duties. Furthermore, federal prosecutors will be enabled and empowered to dismantle criminal organizations and gangs to put violent offenders in prison.

REBUILD
OUR MILITARY

President Trump will push the Restoring National Security Act, which rebuilds our military by expanding military investment. The Act will give veterans the choice of medical providers, instead of dictating they only seek medical attention at the VA. As for national security, America's electric grid is not protected from EMP or enemy hacking as it should be.[38] The **Restoring National Security Act** contains elements that beef up our vital infrastructure to protect it from cyber-attack, and produce better screening procedures to prevent terrorists from entering our country.

ENACT
NEW ETHICS REFORMS
TO REDUCE
CORRUPTION

President Trump will "drain the swamp" with the Clean Up Corruption in Washington Act. This means introducing new ethics reforms that reduce or eliminate the influence of special interests on our political processes. As one poll shows that nearly 9 in 10 Americans believe the rich will always find a way to subvert campaign laws, President Trump wants to return ethics to the Federal Government and regain the trust of the American People.[39]

America's New Dawn by Elizabeth Little & Ellen Sallas
Prints available at MyPresidentStickers.com

REPORT CARD

On the next few pages, record events as President Trump checks off his Contract with the American Voter!

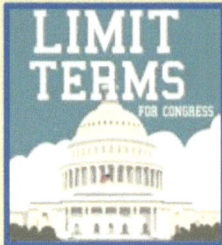

LIMIT TERMS FOR CONGRESS

DATE OF ACTION TAKEN

CHIEF ACTORS

ADDITIONAL NOTES

_____
_____
_____
_____
_____
_____

ONE YEAR LATER

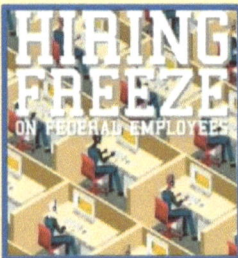

_____
_____
_____

HIRING FREEZE ON FEDERAL EMPLOYEES

DATE OF ACTION TAKEN

CHIEF ACTORS

ADDITIONAL NOTES

_____
_____
_____
_____
_____

ONE YEAR LATER

_____
_____
_____

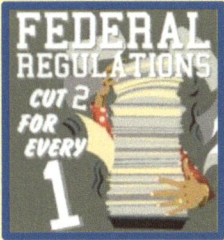

FEDERAL REGULATIONS CUT 2 FOR EVERY 1

DATE OF ACTION TAKEN

CHIEF ACTORS

ADDITIONAL NOTES

_____

_____

_____

_____

_____

_____

ONE YEAR LATER

_____

_____

_____

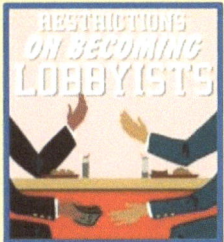

RESTRICTIONS ON BECOMING LOBBYISTS

DATE OF ACTION TAKEN

CHIEF ACTORS

ADDITIONAL NOTES

_____

_____

_____

_____

_____

_____

ONE YEAR LATER

_____

_____

_____

RENEGOTIATE NAFTA

DATE OF ACTION TAKEN

CHIEF ACTORS

ADDITIONAL NOTES

_____

_____

_____

_____

_____

_____

ONE YEAR LATER

_____

_____

_____

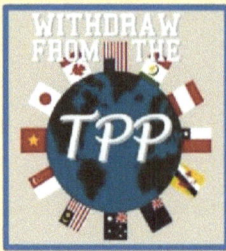

DATE OF ACTION TAKEN

CHIEF ACTORS

ADDITIONAL NOTES

_____
_____
_____
_____
_____

ONE YEAR LATER

_____
_____
_____

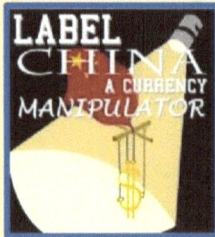

DATE OF ACTION TAKEN

CHIEF ACTORS

ADDITIONAL NOTES

_____
_____
_____
_____
_____

ONE YEAR LATER

_____
_____
_____

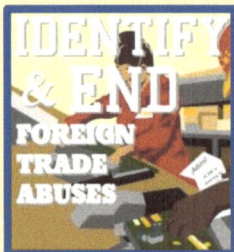

DATE OF ACTION TAKEN

CHIEF ACTORS

ADDITIONAL NOTES

_____
_____
_____
_____
_____

ONE YEAR LATER

_____
_____
_____

LIFT RESTRICTIONS ON U.S. ENERGY RESERVES

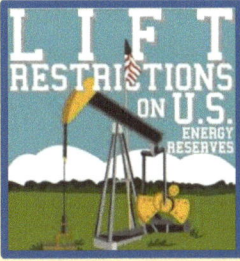

DATE OF ACTION TAKEN

CHIEF ACTORS

ADDITIONAL NOTES

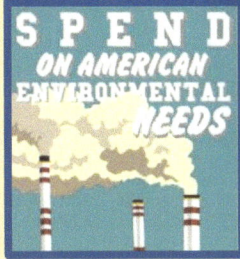

_____
_____
_____
_____
_____
_____

ONE YEAR LATER

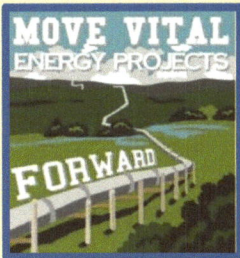

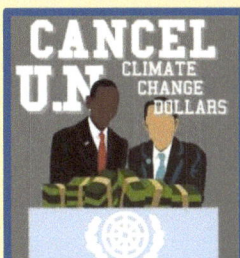

_____
_____
_____

MOVE VITAL ENERGY PROJECTS FORWARD

DATE OF ACTION TAKEN

CHIEF ACTORS

ADDITIONAL NOTES

_____
_____
_____
_____
_____
_____

ONE YEAR LATER

_____
_____
_____

CANCEL U.N CLIMATE CHANGE DOLLARS

SPEND ON AMERICAN ENVIRONMENTAL NEEDS

DATE OF ACTION TAKEN

CHIEF ACTORS

ADDITIONAL NOTES

_____
_____
_____
_____
_____
_____

ONE YEAR LATER

_____
_____
_____

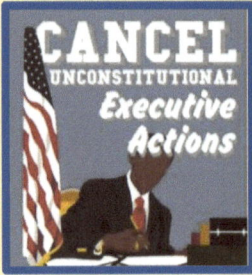

CANCEL UNCONSTITUTIONAL *Executive Actions*

DATE OF ACTION TAKEN

CHIEF ACTORS

ADDITIONAL NOTES

_____

_____

_____

_____

_____

_____

ONE YEAR LATER

_____

_____

_____

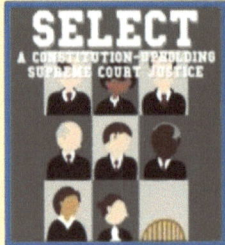

SELECT A CONSTITUTION-UPHOLDING SUPREME COURT JUSTICE

DATE OF ACTION TAKEN

CHIEF ACTORS

ADDITIONAL NOTES

_____

_____

_____

_____

_____

_____

ONE YEAR LATER

_____

_____

_____

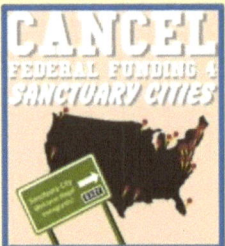

CANCEL FEDERAL FUNDING 4 *SANCTUARY CITIES*

DATE OF ACTION TAKEN

CHIEF ACTORS

ADDITIONAL NOTES

_____

_____

_____

_____

_____

_____

ONE YEAR LATER

_____

_____

_____

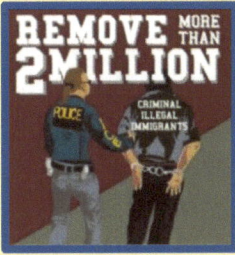

DATE OF ACTION TAKEN

CHIEF ACTORS

ADDITIONAL NOTES

_____
_____
_____
_____
_____
_____

ONE YEAR LATER

_____
_____
_____

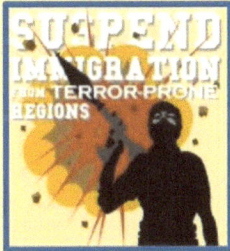

DATE OF ACTION TAKEN

CHIEF ACTORS

ADDITIONAL NOTES

_____
_____
_____
_____
_____
_____

ONE YEAR LATER

_____
_____
_____

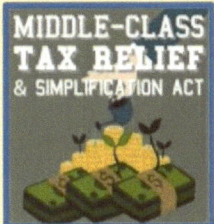

DATE OF ACTION TAKEN

CHIEF ACTORS

ADDITIONAL NOTES

_____
_____
_____
_____
_____
_____
_____

ONE YEAR LATER

_____
_____
_____

END THE OFFSHORING ACT

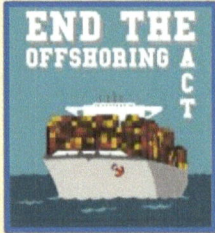

DATE OF ACTION TAKEN

CHIEF ACTORS

ADDITIONAL NOTES

_____

_____

_____

_____

_____

ONE YEAR LATER

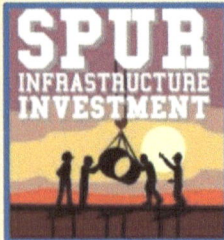

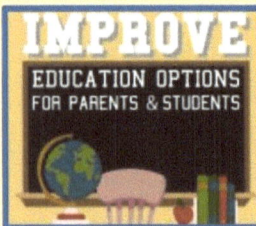

_____

_____

_____

SPUR INFRASTRUCTURE INVESTMENT

DATE OF ACTION TAKEN

CHIEF ACTORS

ADDITIONAL NOTES

_____

_____

_____

_____

_____

ONE YEAR LATER

_____

_____

_____

IMPROVE EDUCATION OPTIONS FOR PARENTS & STUDENTS

DATE OF ACTION TAKEN

CHIEF ACTORS

ADDITIONAL NOTES

_____

_____

_____

_____

_____

ONE YEAR LATER

_____

_____

_____

REPEAL & REPLACE OBAMACARE

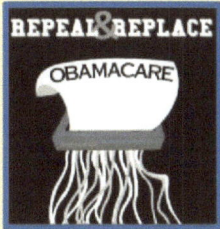

DATE OF ACTION TAKEN

CHIEF ACTORS

ADDITIONAL NOTES

_____
_____
_____
_____
_____
_____

ONE YEAR LATER

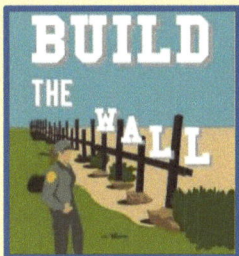

_____
_____
_____

VASTLY IMPROVE CHILD & ELDER CARE TAX DEDUCTIONS

DATE OF ACTION TAKEN

CHIEF ACTORS

ADDITIONAL NOTES

_____
_____
_____
_____
_____
_____

ONE YEAR LATER

_____
_____
_____

BUILD THE WALL

DATE OF ACTION TAKEN

CHIEF ACTORS

ADDITIONAL NOTES

_____
_____
_____
_____
_____
_____

ONE YEAR LATER

_____
_____
_____

REDUCE
CRIME & VIOLENCE
NATIONWIDE

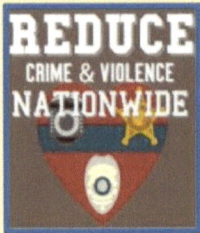

DATE OF ACTION TAKEN

CHIEF ACTORS

ADDITIONAL NOTES

_____
_____
_____
_____
_____
_____

ONE YEAR LATER

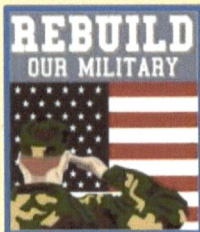

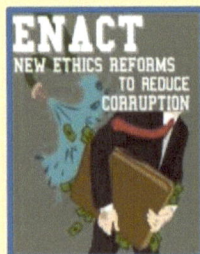

_____
_____
_____

REBUILD
OUR MILITARY

DATE OF ACTION TAKEN

CHIEF ACTORS

ADDITIONAL NOTES

_____
_____
_____
_____
_____
_____

ONE YEAR LATER

_____
_____
_____

ENACT
NEW ETHICS REFORMS
TO REDUCE
CORRUPTION

DATE OF ACTION TAKEN

CHIEF ACTORS

ADDITIONAL NOTES

_____
_____
_____
_____
_____
_____

ONE YEAR LATER

_____
_____
_____

FIRST
100
DAYS
CONTRACT
WITH
AMERICA
COLORING
BOOK

BY ELIZABETH LITTLE
& ELLEN SALLAS

DONAL.

THUMP

#45
POTUS

This book is also available in eBook and as a fun coloring book for kids of all ages, available at booksellers, as well as online.

www.Amazon.com
www.MyPresidentStickers.com
www.EllenCMaze.com

For more information on President Donald Trump's plan to make America great again, please visit WWW.DONALDJTRUMP.COM

Besides the authors' knowledge of United States politics and events, the following resources were considered and consulted when developing this book:

1 - https://www.donaldjtrump.com/press-releases/donald-j.-trump-delivers-groundbreaking-contract-for-the-american-vote1

2 - https://www.reference.com/government-politics/many-times-can-senator-re-elected-87699552cc88218

3 - https://www.termlimits.org/about/

4 - http://www.cnsnews.com/news/article/terence-p-jeffrey/21955000-12329000-government-employees-outnumber-manufacturing

5 - https://www.google.com/#q=federal+employees+bored+at+work

6 - Paraphrased from entire article at https://www.cato.org/policy-report/januaryfebruary-2015/too-many-laws-too-many-costs

7 - https://www.google.com/#q=current+administration+Obama+scandals

8 - https://en.wikipedia.org/wiki/North_American_Free_Trade_Agreement

9 - http://economyincrisis.org/content/why-nafta-is-bad-for-the-u-s

10 - http://www.pri.org/stories/2016-07-26/what-tpp-and-why-are-both-parties-so-angry-about-it

11 - https://www.eff.org/issues/tpp

12 - http://www.slate.com/articles/news_and_politics/explainer/2012/10/china_currency_manipulation_how_does_it_harm_the_u_s_and_what_can_we_do.html

13 - http://www.ndtv.com/world-news/would-label-china-as-currency-manipulator-donald-trump-1459456

14 - Paraphrased from entire article http://www.huffingtonpost.com/leo-w-gerard/trade-abuse_b_7251902.html

15 - http://www.heritage.org/research/reports/2016/09/time-to-unlock-americas-vast-oil-and-gas-resources#_ftn5

16 - http://www.heritage.org/research/reports/2016/09/time-to-unlock-americas-vast-oil-and-gas-resources#_ftn6

17 - http://dailysignal.com/2014/01/31/keystone-xl-pipeline-still-environmentally-safe/

18 - http://www.heritage.org/research/reports/2016/06/the-us-should-withdraw-from-the-united-nations-framework-convention-on-climate-change#_ftn1

19 - http://www.businessinsider.com/us-drought-water-scarcity-2013-5

20 - http://www.popularmechanics.com/technology/infrastructure/g85/4257814/?slide=1

21 - http://www.popularmechanics.com/technology/infrastructure/g85/4257814/?slide=2, http://ny.curbed.com/2016/11/11/13598192/brooklyn-bridge-repairs-cost-increase

22 - http://www.heritage.org/research/reports/2014/02/an-executive-unbound-the-obama-administrations-unilateral-actions

23 - http://abcnews.go.com/blogs/politics/2014/01/obama-says-pen-phone-will-see-action-in-2014/

24 – If the format had allowed for it, the authors would love to have included this closely related QUOTE: "And folks, what happened in this election were all those people out there in the land of God, guns, grits and gravy had it up to here. They didn't sit on their butt on Election Day. They got out of their chairs. They would have gone to vote if it would have been 16 inches of rain. Hillary gave them nothing to vote for and Donald Trump gave them something that they'd been missing for a long time, even among the Republicans and so-called conservatives. He gave them hope that somebody was listening. And somebody would work to restore a sense of pride. And then on that Election Day the folks from the land of God, guns, grits and gravy would not be taking a knee during the National Anthem and Debbie, what a magnificent rendition of that you gave to us tonight. And I observed not one person in this place in their chair or on their knee." Governor Mike Huckabee, November 2016. Transcript and video found at http://www.frontpagemag.com/fpm/264895/gov-mike-huckabee-why-trump-won%C2%A0-frontpagemagcom

25 - http://www.businessinsider.com/where-donald-trump-stands-on-weed-legalization-2016-11

26 - http://www.usnews.com/news/politics/articles/2017-01-04/trumps-double-barreled-supreme-court-nomination-strategy

27 - http://www.rasmussenreports.com/public_content/politics/current_events/immigration/july_2015/voters_want_to_punish_sanctuary_cities

28 - http://www.foxnews.com/politics/2016/08/28/trump-vows-to-deport-criminal-illegal-immigrants-within-one-hour-swearing-in.html

29 - https://en.wikipedia.org/wiki/Global_Terrorism_Index

30 - https://www.donaldjtrump.com/press-releases/donald-j.-trump-delivers-groundbreaking-contract-for-the-american-vote1

31 - https://www.donaldjtrump.com/press-releases/donald-j.-trump-delivers-groundbreaking-contract-for-the-american-vote1

32 - http://www.realclearpolicy.com/articles/2016/10/30/donald_trumps_contract_with_the_american_voter.html

33 - http://www.infrastructurereportcard.org/

34- http://americafirstproject.org/issue/education/

35 - https://assets.donaldjtrump.com/CONTRACT_FOR_THE_VOTER.pdf (End Illegal Immigration Act)

36- http://www.breitbart.com/big-journalism/2015/08/08/illegal-alien-crime-accounts-for-over-30-of-murders-in-some-states/

37 – https://www.fbi.gov/news/stories/latest-crime-statistics-released

38- http://securethegrid.com/the-basics-of-grid-security/

39- http://time.com/4602918/donald-trump-fec-federal-election-commission/

Hand-drawn back cover art with color codes for the graphic artist...

ELLEN SALLAS IS AN AUTHOR AND ILLUSTRATOR FROM CENTRAL ALABAMA. LEARN MORE ABOUT ELLEN AT WWW.ELLENCMAZE.COM

ELIZABETH LITTLE IS A GRAPHIC DESIGNER IN CENTRAL ALABAMA.

MY PRES

#OURMILITARYROCKS

mypresidentstickers.com

T

MY PRESIDENT

(c) ellenemaze.com

Check out what else is fun at Little Roni
www.littleronipublishers.com

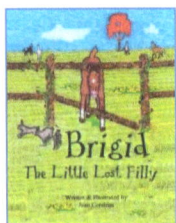

Brigid, the Little Lost Filly (All Ages, 4th Grade RL)
Jean Condren

When Brigid slips out of her pasture home for an adventure in the cornfield on the other side, only when takes the time to stop and think through her problem does she find her way home again.

$14.99, 45 pages, full-color, softcover, ISBN 978-1539126096

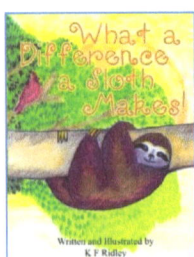

What a Difference a Sloth Makes (All Ages, 2nd Grade RL)
K F Ridley

What makes a sloth so special? The same thing that makes everyone special-- individuality. Beautifully illustrated picture book. You are here for a reason and you are special in your own way. Reading level K-2nd grade.

$12.99, 42 pages, full-color, softcover, ISBN 978-0692631195

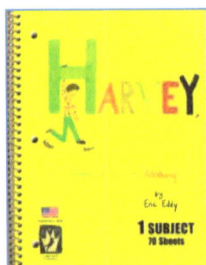

Harvey, Who's Good at Nothing (Ages 6-up, 4th Grade RL)
Eric Eddy

Harvey's homework is to "think of something you are good at". Sounds easy, right? Not for Harvey. He thinks and thinks and thinks, and only sees the skills of everyone else in comparison. Join Harvey as he learns that everyone is good at SOMEthing!

$14.99, 36 pages, full-color, softcover, ISBN 978-0692513002
$4.99 Kindle

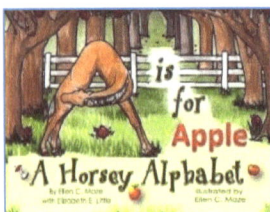

A is for Apple: A Horsey Alphabet (All Ages, 4th Grade RL)
Ellen C. Maze and Elizabeth E. Little

Twenty-six fantastically limber horses bend & twist into each letter of the alphabet and teach alliteration / new words along the way.

$9.50/$.99 Paperback/Kindle.
66 pages, full-color, ISBN 978-0615719450

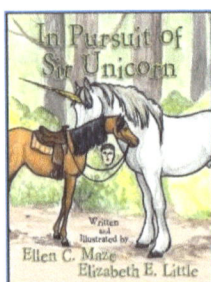

In Pursuit of Sir Unicorn (Ages 6-up, 4th Grade RL)
by Ellen C. Maze and Elizabeth Little

While out on a trail ride on a lovely summer's day, the man and his horse meet a giant unicorn. The adventures that ensue take the man over hill and dale in pursuit of the most elusive of mythical creatures. Will he get his horse back from the unicorn? Read along in rhyming prose and find out!

$12/$2.99 Paperback/Kindle, 46 pages, full-color softcover, ISBN 978-0615778273

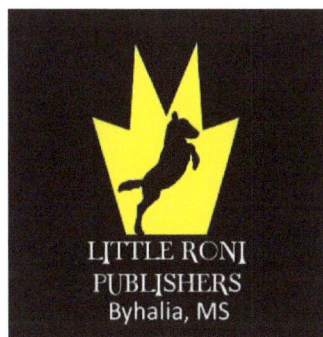

LITTLE RONI
PUBLISHERS
Byhalia, MS

www.LittleRoniPublishers.com

www.ingramcontent.com/pod-product-compliance
Lightning Source LLC
Chambersburg PA
CBHW060856270326
41934CB00003B/167